Treasures
Uncovered

The Parables of Jesus

Treasures Uncovered

The Parables of Jesus

Jeanne Kun

the WORD
among us®

The Word Among Us Press
9639 Doctor Perry Road
Ijamsville, Maryland 21754
www.wordamongus.org

ISBN: 978-1-59325-056-0

Made and printed in the United States of America
12 11 10 09 08   3 4 5 6 7

Cover Design: Evelyn Harris
Text Design: David Crosson

Nihil obstat: The Reverend Michael Morgan, Chancellor
Censor Librorum
May 5, 2005

Imprimatur: +Most Reverend Victor Galeone
Bishop of St. Augustine
May 5, 2005

Scripture citations are taken from the New Revised Standard Version Bible: Catholic
Edition, copyright ©1989, 1993, Division of Christian Education of the National Council
of the Churches of Christ in the United States of America.
Used by permission. All rights reserved.

Excerpts from the English translation of the *Catechism of the Catholic Church*
for use in the United States of America, copyright © 1994, United States Catholic
Conference, Inc. – Libreria Editrice Vaticana. Used with permission.

Library of Congress Cataloging-in-Publication Data

Kun, Jeanne, 1951-
Treasures uncovered : the parables of Jesus / Jeanne Kun.
p. cm. -- (The Word Among Us keys to the Bible)
ISBN 1-59325-056-8 (alk. paper)
1. Jesus Christ--Parables. I. Title. II. Series.
BT375.3.K86 2005
226.8'077--dc22
2005011639

Contents

Welcome to
The Word Among Us
Keys to the Bible

Have you ever lost your keys? Everyone seems to have at least one "lost keys" story to tell. Maybe you had to break a window of your house or wait for the auto club to let you into your car. Whatever you had to do probably cost you—in time, energy, money, or all three. Keys are definitely important items to have on hand!

The guides in The Word Among Us Keys to the Bible series are meant to provide you with a handy set of keys that can "unlock" the treasures of the Scriptures for you. Scripture is God's living word. Within its pages we meet the Lord. So as we study and meditate on Scripture and unlock its many treasures, we discover the riches it contains—and in the process, we grow in intimacy with God.

Since 1982, *The Word Among Us* magazine has helped Catholics develop a deeper relationship with the Lord through daily meditations that bring the Scriptures to life. More than ever, Catholics today desire to read and pray with the Scriptures, and many have begun to form small faith-sharing groups to explore the Bible together.

We recently conducted a survey among our magazine readers to learn what they wanted in a Catholic Bible study. The many enthusiastic responses we received led us to create this new series. Readers told us they are looking for easy-to-understand, faith-filled materials that approach Scripture from a clearly Catholic perspective. Moreover, they want a Bible study that shows them how they can apply what they learn from Scripture to their everyday lives. And since most of our readers lead busy lives, they asked for sessions that they can complete in an hour or two.

On the basis of the survey results, we set out to design a simple, easy-to-use Bible study guide that is also challenging and thought provoking. We hope that this first guide fulfills those admittedly ambitious goals. We are confident, however, that taking the time to go through this guide—whether by yourself, with a friend, or in a small group—will be a worthwhile endeavor that will bear fruit in your life.

If the Bible is a storehouse of treasures, then each book of the Old and New Testament must contain numerous compartments or rooms. In *Treasures Uncovered: The Parables of Jesus,* we will unlock the gospel rooms containing some of Jesus' parables. Exploring these stories can give us valuable insights into Jesus' own heart and mind—insights that will move us to a deeper love for him and a greater desire to do his will.

How to Use the Guides in This Series

The study guides in the Keys to the Bible series are divided into six sessions that each deal with a particular aspect of the topic. Before starting the first session, take time to read the introduction, which contains helpful background information on the Scripture texts to be studied. It will provide the foundation for the six sessions that follow. In this guide, the introduction examines the role of parables in Jesus' ministry, while each session focuses on one or two specific parables.

Whether you use this guide for personal reflection and study, as part of a faith-sharing group, or as an aid in your prayer time, be sure to begin each session with prayer. Ask God to open his word to you and to speak to you personally. Read each Scripture passage slowly and carefully. Then, take as much time as you need to meditate on the story and pursue any thoughts it brings to mind. When you are ready, move on to the accompanying commentary, which offers various insights into the text.

Two sets of questions are included in each session to help you "mine" the Scripture passage and discover its relevance to your life. Those under the heading "Understand!" focus on the text itself and help you grasp what it means. Occasionally a question allows for a variety of answers and is meant to help you explore the passage from several angles. "Grow!" questions are intended to elicit a personal response by helping you examine your life in light of the values and truths that you uncover through your study of the Scripture passage and its setting. Under the headings "Reflect!" and "Act!" we offer suggestions to help you respond concretely to the challenges posed by the passage.

Finally, pertinent quotations from the Fathers of the Church as well as insights from contemporary writers appear throughout each session. Coupled with relevant selections from the *Catechism of the Catholic Church* and information about the history, geography, and culture of first-century Palestine, these selections (called "In the Spotlight") can add new layers of understanding and insight to your study.

As is true with any other learning resource, you will benefit the most from this study by writing your answers to the questions in the spaces provided. The simple act of writing can help you formulate your thoughts more clearly—and it will also give you a record of your reflections and spiritual growth that you can return to in the future to see how much God has accomplished in your life. End your reading or study with a prayer thanking God for what you have learned—and ask the Holy Spirit to guide you in living out the call you have been given as a Christian in the world today.

Although the Scripture passages to be studied and the related verses for your reflection are printed in full in each guide (from the New Revised Standard Version: Catholic Edition), you will find it helpful to have a Bible on hand for looking up other passages and cross-references or comparing different translations.

The format of the guides in The Word Among Us Keys to the Bible series is especially well suited for use in small groups. Some recommendations and practical tips for using this guide in a Bible discussion group are offered on pages 102–105.

As you use this book to unlock Jesus' parables and discover the spiritual treasures contained in them, may the Holy Spirit draw you closer to Jesus, increase your love for him, and widen your vision of his kingdom.

The Word Among Us Press

Introduction
Discovering the Treasures in Jesus' Parables

As we read the stories in the gospels, we often form a mental picture of Jesus as he went about his mission. Perhaps we imagine him sitting in a boat, speaking to the crowds that have gathered on the shore to listen to him. Or we might visualize him standing on a hillside, surrounded by huge numbers of people who are jostling one another in their eagerness to secure a spot near this extraordinary rabbi from Galilee. These scenes are easy for us to envision because we're so familiar with the gospel accounts of Jesus and his ministry.

But have you ever wondered what Jesus actually sounded like when he spoke? We don't know whether his voice was deep and resonant or had a mellow timbre, yet surely the tones in which he spoke reinforced the meaning of his words. We'd hardly imagine Jesus rebuking demons in a soft-spoken manner. And when he forgave sinners and consoled the sick, the warmth of his voice must have conveyed tenderness and compassion.

Jesus' words are still loud and clear today, although his voice is no longer audible. And among the words of Jesus that resonate in our minds and hearts most strongly are those contained in the striking parables he told.

"Why Do You Speak in Parables?"

Jesus was a storyteller par excellence. Stories like those of the good Samaritan, the Pharisee and the tax collector, and the prodigal son have become ingrained in our culture. Lost sheep and pearls of great price are catalogued in our mental file of symbolic images. For generations of Christians and non-Christians alike, the parables Jesus told have served as metaphors for our collective conscience.

Speaking in parables was a characteristic feature of Jesus' teaching, both to his own disciples and to those who flocked to hear him. He presented the truths of his kingdom through parables—"earthly stories with heavenly meanings," as they have been popularly called—not to entertain his listeners but to instruct them.

"Parable" is derived from *para* and *bolé*, two Greek words that literally mean "something thrown or placed alongside something else." The Hebrew counterpart to "parable" is *mashal*, a term that broadly encompasses such figures and forms of speech as similes, analogies, metaphors, proverbs, riddles, and stories. Examples range from one-line sayings—"You are the light of the world" (Matthew 5:14)—to long illustrative stories like the parable of the sower (Luke 8:4-15) and dramatic narratives like the one about the unrighteous steward (16:1-13).

Whatever their length, parables make comparisons to show how similar or different things are. In much the same way that metaphors work, parables describe concepts that are unfamiliar or intangible *in terms of* concepts that are familiar, vivid, and concrete. The effect is that we transfer characteristics and opinions of objects, events, or situations that we understand to those that are abstract or less familiar to us. In the parables, Jesus often helped his listeners understand what God expected of them through narratives of events in this world: "The kingdom of heaven may be compared to a king who gave a wedding banquet . . ." (Matthew 22:2). In telling these stories, Jesus drew upon ordinary objects and images, such as seed and salt, lamps and leaven, to communicate spiritual principles. As he told his followers, "From the fig tree learn its lesson" (Mark 13:28). He spoke the language of the people and used parables to make his message accessible to everyone.

What makes the parables different from other types of metaphor is that they don't merely compare two individual objects or events. Rather, the situations in the stories Jesus told provide insight into moral principles with broad applications. So, while the elements of the individual parables were drawn from particular situations that could have occurred in that culture and at that point in history, their subjects are universal themes that transcend cultures and time. The spiritual truths they contain about life, death, God, and human relationships resonate with all of human existence. The fact that the parables still speak to us today is evidence of their enduring nature.

Moreover, Jesus frequently underscored spiritual truths of the parables through the use of hyperbole and by contrasting opposite qualities such as virtue and vice, wisdom and foolishness, generosity and meanness of spirit. The parable of the rich man and poor Lazarus (Luke 16:19-31) is an animated portrayal of just such a contrast. And there is no clearer instance of exaggeration than the parable of the unforgiving servant, in which a slave who was forgiven for a debt of 150,000 years' wages refused to forgive a debt against him for only a hundred days' wages (Matthew 18:23-35).

That is not to say that the meaning of all of the parables was immediately apparent. Even the apostles frequently had to ask Jesus to explain them. Like the best novels and poems written by human authors, these divine stories have multiple layers of meaning and interpretation. For Jesus' first-century audience as for us today, they are capable of teaching moral truths, sparking new insights, and deepening our understanding of God and our faith.

"Explain to Us the Parable"

Why was speaking in parables one of Jesus' favorite teaching methods? Telling a story is a powerful means of capturing people's attention. A gifted storyteller has the ability to gain listeners' interest, involve them in the story's drama, and hold them in suspense regarding its outcome. In addition, the pictorial language of parables and stories is easier to remember than abstract thoughts. Thus, Jesus' vivid parables function to fix chosen concepts and values firmly in our memory and imagination.

Jesus' parables are not simply good or engaging stories—they are stories that are part of God's revelation to us. The love of God, mercy and forgiveness, and the values of the kingdom are among the great themes of Jesus' teaching that he addressed by means of parables. In telling parables, Jesus revealed the heart of God and made his Father's will known to us.

Jesus didn't use his parables to enter into debate or argument with his listeners. But to make a point or explain the principles of God's kingdom, he often posed challenging questions before beginning his parables. "Which one of you . . . ?" (Luke 15:4); "What do you think?" (Matthew 21:28). Sometimes the question came at the end of the story: "Which of these three, do you think, was a neighbor to the man who fell into the hands of the robbers?" (Luke 10:36).

By questioning his hearers, Jesus drew them into the story and challenged them to figure out the message of the parable themselves—often by examining their own hearts and lives and reconsidering their conventional viewpoints or preconceived ideas. Above all, his parables were meant to evoke a personal response that would have consequences in each hearer's life: They were to lead his audience to conversion, to a change in their attitude or behavior toward God and one another. "Words are not enough; deeds are required. The parables are like mirrors for man: will he be hard soil or good earth for the word?" (*Catechism of the Catholic Church,* 546). Our heavenly Father speaks to us through Jesus' stories and calls us, through the promptings of the Holy Spirit, to a reorientation and transformation of our lives. We are not to remain passive hearers.

Frequently Jesus' parables are provoking and paradoxical. Quite often their conclusions are surprising. Sometimes the choice of characters and their roles confound expectations. The opening of the parable arouses interest; as the story unfolds, the problem or issue emerges and suspense mounts. The climax and resolution may not only be unexpected but even disturbing, unsettling, or irritating—forcing the listeners to confront their own reactions. In some instances, Jesus even leaves the parable open ended, compelling his hearers to finish the story for themselves. For example, we might wonder whether the elder son ever had a change of heart, set aside his resentment, and joined in the celebration for his prodigal brother.

The Written Record

We should remember that Jesus' parables were delivered "on the spot," directed to his listeners in the various circumstances in which he encountered them. He seized "teachable moments" to address the crowds that followed him. Originally spontaneous oral teachings, the parables of Jesus were first passed on among the earliest Christians by word of mouth. Then the gospel Evangelists, relying on their own memories and the testimony and recollections of firsthand witnesses, wrote down the sayings and teachings of Jesus under the inspiration of the Holy Spirit.

In recounting Jesus' parables, the Evangelists would have probably used the original settings in which they were told, if those were known. Or, they may have provided a framework suited to the content and sense of Jesus' teachings as well as to the thrust and structure of the gospel as a whole. The pastoral concerns of the early church also affected how the parables were recorded and interpreted in the gospels. For example, the lost sheep in the parable in the Gospel of Luke (15:4-7) is descriptive of sinners Jesus welcomed, whereas in Matthew 18:12-14, the "sheep gone astray" is identified with fallen-away Christians in need of special care by the church community.

Such applications of Jesus' parables should not be seen as misrepresentations or distortions of his original meaning. Rather, they indicate how the Evangelists and the early church, under the guidance of the Holy Spirit, recognized the living quality of Jesus' words and their relevance to every generation that hears them.

"Let Anyone with Ears Listen!"

Understanding and interpreting Jesus' parables often demands some real effort, but delving deep enough to uncover their riches and treasures has its own rewards. Most of the parables are multi-layered and cannot be reduced to a single lesson or message. Such oversimplification would strip the stories of their mystery and severely limit their impact. On the other hand, Jesus' parables are not allegories in which every detail in the story has a particular hidden significance and needs to be analyzed and broken like a secret code. Though many of the parables do contain allegorical features and images that serve as symbols of divine realities, attempting a point-by-point analytical interpretation of each detail has often led to some strange stretching of the imagination.

If grasping the parables demands effort, allowing them to transform us requires not only hard work but open, willing hearts. We can understand Jesus' stories and integrate their truths into our lives only when we desire to be close to God—when we welcome his words with faith, yearn to do his will, and surrender ourselves to him in love. Perhaps that's why Jesus told his disciples that the "secrets of the kingdom of heaven" are not given to all (Matthew 13:11) and so often declared, "Let anyone with ears listen!" (Matthew 13:9, 43; Luke 8:8).

Another way to "hear" Jesus' parables is to read them aloud. Words come alive—and call forth life—when we give them voice. In earlier centuries, people normally read aloud; reading silently is actually a fairly modern development. Although we often hear Jesus' parables proclaimed in the Liturgy of the Word, it may be helpful to try reading them aloud by yourself or within your faith-sharing group. By reading them with expression, you may gain new insights. Such a practice can restore to the written word its original spoken quality and help you and your group imagine that you are there, at the scene, listening to Jesus speak.

As you progress through this guide, may you uncover all the treasures the Lord has for you, especially the "pearl of great price"—Jesus himself. As you listen to his words, may your love for him increase so that your heart's desire is to give all that you have to "purchase" that precious pearl.

Jeanne Kun

"Go and Do Likewise"

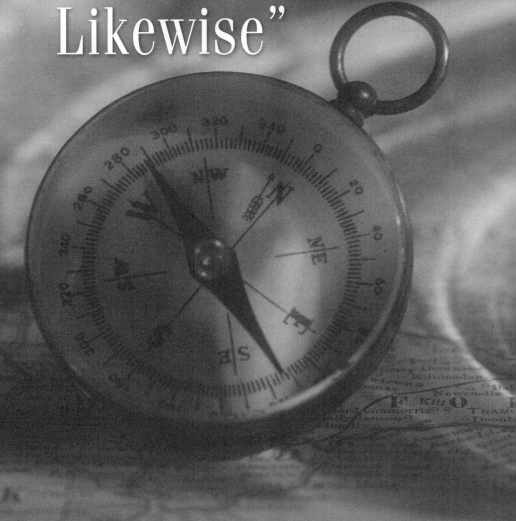

Luke 10:25-37

²⁵ Just then a lawyer stood up to test Jesus. "Teacher," he said, "what must I do to inherit eternal life?" ²⁶He said to him, "What is written in the law? What do you read there?" ²⁷He answered, "You shall love the Lord your God with all your heart, and with all your soul, and with all your strength, and with all your mind; and your neighbor as yourself." ²⁸And he said to him, "You have given the right answer; do this, and you will live."

²⁹ But wanting to justify himself, he asked Jesus, "And who is my neighbor?" ³⁰Jesus replied, "A man was going down from Jerusalem to Jericho, and fell into the hands of robbers, who stripped him, beat him, and went away, leaving him half dead. ³¹Now by chance a priest was going down that road; and when he saw him, he passed by on the other side. ³²So likewise a Levite, when he came to the place and saw him, passed by on the other side. ³³But a Samaritan while traveling came near him; and when he saw him, he was moved with pity. ³⁴He went to him and bandaged his wounds, having poured oil and wine on them. Then he put him on his own animal, brought him to an inn, and took care of him. ³⁵The next day he took out two denarii, gave them to the innkeeper, and said, 'Take care of him; and when I come back, I will repay you whatever more you spend.' ³⁶Which of these three, do you think, was a neighbor to the man who fell into the hands of the robbers?" ³⁷He said, "The one who showed him mercy." Jesus said to him, "Go and do likewise."

> The present imperatives "go" and "do" imply that Jesus commands the lawyer (and the listener/reader) to go and put this into effect by following the example of the Samaritan, not by a single act but by lifelong conduct.
> —Herman Hendrickx, CICM, *The Parables of Jesus*

When the lawyer asked Jesus, "Who is my neighbor?" he really wanted to know where to draw the line. The law's command is to "love your neighbor as yourself" (Leviticus 19:18; Matthew 22:39). Whether any but fellow Jews qualified as their "neighbors" was much debated by first-century Jews, and many believed that gentiles and nonbelievers were excluded from that category. Thus, the underlying question posed by the lawyer was, "Just how far do my obligations extend?"

Jesus didn't answer the lawyer directly. Instead, he told a story about neighborliness that transcended the original question and showed the lawyer what it really means to fulfill the law of love.

A master storyteller, Jesus knew well how to use the element of surprise. Jews viewed Samaritans as apostates, people who rejected the faith, and there was deep enmity between the two groups (2 Kings 17:24-41; Matthew 10:5; Luke 9:52-55; John 4:9). Any Jewish listener—including the lawyer who posed the question—would have typecast a Samaritan as the villain. But Jesus didn't cast the Samaritan as one of the robbers. Nor did he even make the Samaritan the victim, in order to show these Jews that they had a duty to love even a person like that. Such a story may have succeeded in transforming their outward behavior toward people they despised—but it would have failed in Jesus' deeper objective of transforming their hearts.

Instead, Jesus confounded his listeners' expectations by making the Samaritan the very model of neighborly behavior that they should seek to emulate. The priest and the Levite—not only Jews like Jesus' listeners, but also experts in the law and exemplars of character—saw the injured man but didn't stop to help. Only the Samaritan demonstrated real love, by going out of his way to tend to the unfortunate man's wounds and provide for his care. By portraying the Samaritan as the hero, Jesus shattered the preconceived notions of the Jews in his audience, challenging them to learn from a Samaritan what it really means to love. And not only did Jesus show this audience that everyone deserves their love, he revealed that someone they perceived as an enemy was also capable of loving them.

Why didn't the priest or the Levite help the man who had fallen among robbers? Jesus doesn't reveal their reasons for inaction, but leaves it to his listeners to guess. Perhaps the priest and the Levite hurried past out of fear that they could become the robbers' next victims. Or perhaps they reasoned that the man was already dead, and so not only would they be of no help, but touching the corpse would have made them ritually unclean and thus unfit to perform their temple service (Leviticus 21:1). But since neither of them even came close enough to see whether the man was dead or alive, a more likely conclusion is that—despite their religious standing—they simply didn't have any compassion. Or, as we would say today, they just "didn't want to get involved."

It was the despised Samaritan who was so moved with compassion at the sight of the wounded man that he took the chance to "get involved." Selfless love and mercy motivated him to do all he could for a fellow human being in distress, no matter the inconvenience, the cost, or the risk to himself.

Like the people in Jesus' audience, we are called to a love without prejudice or limit, a love that recognizes the dignity of every person and reflects the love our heavenly Father has for us, his sons and daughters. When Jesus asked which of the three was a neighbor to the man who had been attacked, the inquiring lawyer correctly replied, "The one who showed him mercy." Jesus' message to us is the same today as it was to the inquiring lawyer so many years ago: "Go and do likewise" (Luke 10:37).

Understand!

1. Why do you think the lawyer wanted to "test" Jesus (Luke 10: 25)? Imagine the various ways the lawyer might have responded to Jesus' choice of a Samaritan as the hero of the parable.

_____

_____

_____

_____

_____

_____

2. Jesus did not identify the wounded man in the parable in any way. What does this suggest to you?

_____

_____

_____

_____

_____

_____

3. List all the verbs that describe the Samaritan's actions toward the wounded man. Why, in your opinion, did Jesus detail the Samaritan's actions so explicitly as he told this parable?

_____

_____

_____

_____

_____

_____

4. What did the Samaritan's acts of kindness cost him (besides the money he paid to the innkeeper)? What risks did he take by helping the wounded man? What do his actions suggest about his character?

_____

_____

_____

_____

_____

5. How does this parable add to your understanding of Jesus? Of the characteristics of his kingdom? Of his conception of love and mercy?

_____

_____

_____

_____

_____

▶ In the Spotlight
The Path of Blood

Jerusalem rises 2,700 feet above sea level, while Jericho, located near the Dead Sea, lies 820 feet below sea level—a difference in elevation of about 3,500 feet. Although the steep road linking the two cities was heavily traveled by pilgrims and caravans, it was extremely treacherous nonetheless. Covering a distance of seventeen miles, it crossed rocky deserts, wound around limestone outcrops and cliffs, and squeezed through narrow gullies. Because of the difficulty involved in traversing such rough, desolate terrain, as well as the constant danger of being ambushed by thieves, the road between Jerusalem and Jericho became known as "the path of blood."

Grow!

1. Recall times in your life when you acted like the priest or the Levite. What caused you to pass by someone in need? Now recall a time when you acted like the Samaritan. What caused you to respond differently?

   _____

   _____

   _____

   _____

   _____

2. How would a greater awareness of the needs of others help you to become a more compassionate person? What practical steps could you take to help those who are homeless, poor, lonely, or mentally or physically impaired?

   _____

   _____

   _____

   _____

   _____

3. Who has "poured wine and oil" on your wounds, caring for you in times of difficulty or need? What aspect of their help did you value most? Why? What did their kindness toward you teach you about how you should reach out to others?

   _____

   _____

   _____

   _____

4. Why is loving and caring for others essential to maintaining a loving relationship with God (1 John 4:20-21)? How is your love for others a witness to your faith in Christ?

_____

_____

_____

_____

_____

_____

5. In what ways do you limit your love to particular people? In prayer, ask the Holy Spirit how you can overcome any obstacles you may face in loving others as Jesus loves you.

_____

_____

_____

_____

_____

_____

▶ In the Spotlight
A Shift in Perspective

I was a college student on my first visit to another country. It was past midnight, and I was on the last train speeding out of Paris toward the suburbs where my French hosts lived—or so I thought, until I learned I had taken the wrong train. The platform at the end of the line was desolate, with no phones or taxi stands in evidence. My fellow travelers disappeared into the night, too busy to help, and my spirits were at low ebb when I noticed a light in the conductor's window. Seeing the features and skin tone of the man who turned at my knock, however,

I admit that my heart sank. This conductor was an Algerian immigrant. I had never met an Algerian before, but my French friends had warned me to be wary.

This Algerian undid the prejudices I had picked up. He was an angel in disguise. Moved by my plight, he offered to drive me home—an hour out of his way. Quite imprudently, I accepted. ("Never take a ride from a stranger" is still wise advice.)

"Can I at least pay you for the gas?" I asked as he deposited me safely at my doorstep. "No," my rescuer replied. "Just remember this next time you hear someone speaking badly about Algerians."

I never forgot my "angel" or the lesson I learned. Much later I realized that the experience had also taught me something about reading the parables in general, and one parable in particular.

At various times I had reflected on "the good Samaritan." Mostly I had identified with the Samaritan, trying to see how in my own circumstances I might imitate his mercy. At times, passing derelicts on the street or remembering the starving millions of the world, I had felt like the priest and Levite. Not till that night outside Paris had I ever seen myself as the wounded traveler rescued by an outsider. Having also received mercy from an unexpected source, I now began to consider the parable from this angle. *Did the traveler recover?* I wondered. *Was he stunned to discover that it was an enemy who had tended to him? Did his view of Samaritans change?* Shifting my perspective opened up a whole new way to view the story.
—**Louise Perrotta,** "The Grace to Be Taken by Surprise"

Reflect!

1. Meditate on how, over your lifetime, you have grown in loving God with all your heart, soul, mind, and might (Deuteronomy 6:5; Matthew 22:37). Can you recall specific circumstances or experiences that helped to deepen your love for God?

2. Read and reflect on the following passages to enrich your understanding of the parable you have just studied:

> [Jesus said:] "When the Son of Man comes in his glory, and all the angels with him, then he will sit on the throne of his glory. All the nations will be gathered before him, and he will separate people one from another as a shepherd separates the sheep from the goats, and he will put the sheep at his right hand and the goats at the left. Then the king will say to those at his right hand, 'Come, you that are blessed by my Father, inherit the kingdom prepared for you from the foundation of the world; for I was hungry and you gave me food, I was thirsty and you gave me something to drink, I was a stranger and you welcomed me, I was naked and you gave me clothing, I was sick and you took care of me, I was in prison and you visited me.' Then the righteous will answer him, 'Lord, when was it that we saw you hungry and gave you food, or thirsty and gave you something to drink? And when was it that we saw you a stranger and welcomed you, or naked and gave you clothing? And when was it that we saw you sick or in prison and visited you?' And the king will answer them, 'Truly I tell you, just as you did it to one of the least of these who are members of my family, you did it to me.'" (Matthew 25:31-40)

Owe no one anything except to love one another; for the one who loves another has fulfilled the law. The commandments, "You shall not commit adultery; You shall not murder; You shall not steal; You shall not covet"; and any other commandment, are summed up in this word, "Love your neighbor as yourself." Love does no wrong to a neighbor; therefore, love is the fulfilling of the law. (Romans 13:8-10)

[T]he whole law is summed up in a single commandment, "You shall love your neighbor as yourself." (Galatians 5:14)

Let each of you look not to your own interests, but to the interests of others. (Philippians 2:4)

Those who say, "I love God," and hate their brothers and sisters, are liars; for those who do not love a brother or sister whom they have seen, cannot love God whom they have not seen. The commandment we have from him is this: those who love God must love their brothers and sisters also. (1 John 4:20-21)

▶ In the Spotlight
"He Was Moved with Pity"

Esplanchnisthe is the Greek expression frequently used in the gospels to describe the Lord's compassionate disposition. Jesus "was moved with pity" when he cleansed a leper (Mark 1:41) and opened the eyes of the blind men (Matthew 20:34). He "had compassion" when he healed the sick (14:14), raised the widow's son from the dead (Luke 7:13-15), fed the hungry (Matthew 15:32; Mark 8:2), and taught the crowds who gathered to hear him (Mark 6:34).

The word appears only three times in the New Testament in reference to persons other than Jesus who showed compassion or pity: the good Samaritan (Luke 10:33), the father of the prodigal son (15:20), and the master who forgave his servant's debt (Matthew 18:27). In each case, an overwhelming feeling of sympathy for another was the impetus for their compassionate actions.

The root of the verb *esplanchnisthe* is related to the noun *splanchnon*—translated as "innards"—which was recognized in some ancient cultures as the seat of emotions and sympathy. The term "heart" has a similar meaning for us today.

Act!

This week reach out to someone in need, putting into practice one of the "corporal works of mercy": feeding the hungry, visiting the sick and the imprisoned, and providing clothing and shelter for the needy and homeless.

▶ In the Spotlight
Wisdom from the Church Fathers

Some think that their neighbor is their brother, family, relative, or their kinsman. Our Lord teaches who our neighbor is in the gospel parable of a certain man going down from Jerusalem to Jericho. . . . Everyone is our neighbor, and we should not harm anyone. If, on the contrary, we understand our fellow human beings to be only our brothers and relatives, is it then permissible to do evil to strangers? God forbid such a belief! We are neighbors, all people to all people, for we have one Father.
—St. Jerome, *Homily on Psalm 14 (15)*

The Samaritan "who took pity on the man who had fallen among thieves" . . . showed that he was the man's neighbor more by deed than word. According to the passage that says, "Be imitators of me, as I too am of Christ," it is possible for us to imitate Christ and to pity those who "have fallen among thieves." We can go to them, bind their wounds, pour in oil and wine, put them on our own animals, bear their burdens. The Son of God encourages us to do things like this. He is speaking not so much to the teacher of the law as to us and to everyone when he says, "Go and do likewise." If we do, we will receive eternal life in Christ Jesus, to whom is glory and power for ages of ages.
—Origen, *Homilies on the Gospel of Luke*

"Rejoice with Me"

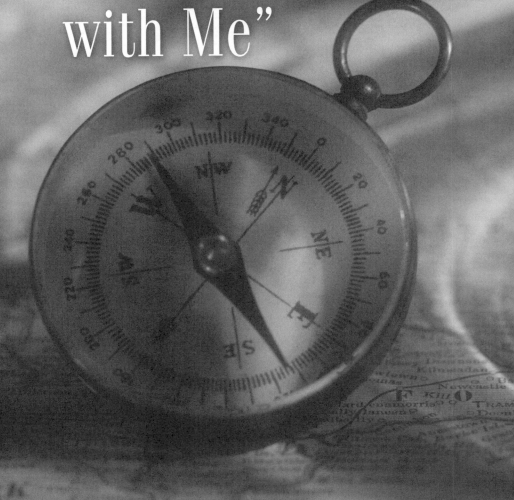

Luke 15:1-7

¹ Now all the tax collectors and sinners were coming near to listen to [Jesus]. ²And the Pharisees and the scribes were grumbling and saying, "This fellow welcomes sinners and eats with them."

³ So he told them this parable: ⁴"Which one of you, having a hundred sheep and losing one of them, does not leave the ninety-nine in the wilderness and go after the one that is lost until he finds it? ⁵When he has found it, he lays it on his shoulders and rejoices. ⁶And when he comes home, he calls together his friends and neighbors, saying to them, 'Rejoice with me, for I have found my sheep that was lost.' ⁷Just so, I tell you, there will be more joy in heaven over one sinner who repents than over ninety-nine righteous persons who need no repentance."

(See also Matthew 18:10-14.)

This parable highlights the joy of Christ and of our heavenly Father at every sinner who repents. God's love is a love that searches us out. It is a love that saves. This is the love that we find in the heart of Jesus.
—**Pope John Paul II,** *Homily at Mass at the Trans World Dome*

The prophet Ezekiel pictured Yahweh as a shepherd caring for Israel, his scattered flock:

> For thus says the Lord GOD: I myself will search for my sheep, and will seek them out. As shepherds seek out their flocks when they are among their scattered sheep, so I will seek out my sheep. . . . I will seek the lost, and I will bring back the strayed, and I will bind up the injured, and I will strengthen the weak. (Ezekiel 34:11-12, 16)

Drawing on this biblical tradition, Jesus used the image of a shepherd searching for his lost sheep to describe God's love for those who have strayed. No one listening to this parable would have found it difficult to identify the straying sheep—they were the very people with whom Jesus was associating.

This wasn't the only time Jesus countered criticism from the Pharisees for embracing sinners and outcasts. On one occasion, Jesus told them, "Those who are well have no need of a physician, but those who are sick; I have come to call not the righteous but sinners" (Mark 2:15-17). Certainly the Pharisees must have been shocked by Jesus' portrayal of a God who welcomed "sinners" before them: "I tell you, the tax collectors and the prostitutes are going into the kingdom of God ahead of you" (Matthew 21:31-32). How startling it must have been to them when Jesus declared that it was his mission "to seek out and to save the lost" (Luke 19:10)!

In this parable of the lost sheep, Jesus underscored the immense value God places on each individual. Only one sheep was lost out of a flock of one hundred. From a practical standpoint, the shepherd may have been wise to "cut his losses" by staying with the ninety-nine. Yet, he diligently seeks out his wayward sheep. Rather than being irritated or angry, the shepherd shows special care for the weak, the lost, and the broken. Each sheep is dear to him simply because it belongs to him, and the loss of even one in a hundred grieves him. The security and well-being of the whole flock is assured by the shepherd's willingness to look for any wandering sheep.

The shepherd doesn't give up his search until he finds the stray that he knows cannot find its way back to the flock without his help. Then he lifts the sheep to his shoulders—an endearing image of closeness and affection—and carries it safely home. The fact is that no one is excluded from God's search. No one is beyond the reaches of his love and mercy. The lost is found, the straying safe again, the sinner saved. Indeed, Jesus himself is the shepherd who cares for us and restores us to friendship with God (John 10:11-18).

This parable reveals the heart of God toward every one of his "lost sheep." And who among us is not lost in some way? Even when we have been "found," how difficult it often is to imagine that God is rejoicing over us. And yet, as Jesus tells the story, the shepherd invited his friends and neighbors to celebrate with him because the sheep that had gone astray was restored to his flock. "Rejoice with me, for I have found my sheep that was lost" (Luke 15:6). With these words, God rejoices with his heavenly court over every repentant sinner he has called back to himself!

> And who among us is not lost in some way? Even when we have been "found," how difficult it often is to imagine that God is rejoicing over us.

Understand!

1. How would you characterize the setting and atmosphere in which Jesus told this parable? In what ways does the setting help you to understand its meaning?

_____

_____

_____

_____

_____

2. Choose three adjectives that describe the shepherd who searches for the lost sheep. How do they reflect your own experience of God?

_____

_____

_____

_____

3. What does this parable reveal about the Pharisees and how they thought of themselves? What does it reveal about God's nature? About Jesus' mission?

_____

_____

_____

_____

_____

4. Note all the verbs used to describe the actions of the shepherd. Which one of these actions speaks most strongly to you? Why?

_____

_____

_____

_____

_____

_____

5. In John 10:11-18, Jesus identifies himself as the good shepherd. How does his description of himself compare to the shepherd in the parable of the lost sheep? In what ways does Jesus go beyond the efforts of the shepherd in the parable?

_____

_____

_____

_____

_____

▶ In the Spotlight
Contemporary Voices

From the beginning of my pontificate, my thoughts, prayers, and actions were motivated by one desire: to witness that Christ, the good shepherd, is present and active in his church. He is constantly searching for every stray sheep, to lead it back to the sheepfold, to bind up its wounds; he tends the sheep that are weak and sickly and protects those that are strong.

—**Pope John Paul II,** *Homily on the 25th Anniversary of His Pontificate*

What must we do? We must imitate the good shepherd and give ourselves without rest for the salvation of souls. Without forgetting material charity and social justice, we must be convinced that the most sublime charity is spiritual charity, that is, the commitment for the salvation of souls. And souls are saved with prayer and sacrifice. This is the mission of the church!
—**Pope John Paul II,** *Homily to the Poor Clares of Albano*

Grow!

1. Recall an occasion when you felt that God was seeking you out. (He may have been acting through another person, through Scripture, or even through a set of circumstances.) Did you welcome his initiative or hesitate to respond to it? Why did you react as you did?

_____

_____

_____

_____

_____

_____

2. Why do you think many people find it difficult to believe that God rejoices when they turn to him in repentance? What underlying attitudes—such as unworthiness, fear, or shame—might prevent you from believing that God is happy to welcome you back?

_____

_____

_____

_____

_____

_____

3. What is your attitude toward people whose behavior is sinful or disreputable? How does Jesus' example help you to overcome any negative attitudes?

_____

_____

_____

_____

_____

_____

_____

4. When have you acted like the shepherd in the parable, reaching out to someone who was in some way lost, wounded, or in need of protection? What happened?

_____

_____

_____

_____

_____

_____

_____

5. Think of a time when you rejoiced in another person's repentance or change of heart. What made you so happy?

_____

_____

_____

_____

_____

_____

_____

▶ In the Spotlight
Wisdom from the Church Fathers

Let us rejoice that the sheep that had strayed in Adam is lifted on Christ. The shoulders of Christ are the arms of the cross. There, I laid down my sins. I rested on the neck of that noble yoke. . . . "The Son of Man came to seek and save what was lost." He sought all, because "as in Adam all men die, so also in Christ shall all be made alive."

—**St. Ambrose,** *Exposition of the Gospel of Luke*

And when he found the sheep, he lays it on his shoulders, rejoicing. He laid the sheep on his shoulders because when he took on our human nature he himself bore our sins. . . . We must notice that he does not say, "Rejoice with the sheep that has been found," but *Rejoice with me.* Our lives are his joy. When we are brought back to heaven, we complete the solemn festival of his delight.

—**St. Gregory the Great,** *Homily 34*

Reflect!

1. Imagine that Jesus is celebrating with you and your family or friends. What event would you choose to celebrate? How might you spend this time together, and what might you say to one another?

2. Reflect on the following passages to enhance your understanding of the parable you have just studied:

> He will feed his flock like a shepherd;
>   he will gather the lambs in his arms,

and carry them in his bosom,
    and gently lead the mother sheep. (Isaiah 40:11)

All we like sheep have gone astray;
    we have all turned to our own way. (Isaiah 53:6)

Sing aloud, O daughter Zion;
    shout, O Israel!
Rejoice and exult with all your heart,
    O daughter Jerusalem!
The LORD has taken away the judgments against you. . . .
[H]e will rejoice over you with gladness,
    he will renew you in his love;
he will exult over you with loud singing
    as on a day of festival. (Zephaniah 3:14-15, 17-18)

[Jesus said:] "I am the good shepherd. The good shepherd lays down his life for the sheep. The hired hand, who is not the shepherd and does not own the sheep, sees the wolf coming and leaves the sheep and runs away—and the wolf snatches them and scatters them. The hired hand runs away because a hired hand does not care for the sheep. I am the good shepherd. I know my own and my own know me, just as the Father knows me and I know the Father. And I lay down my life for the sheep." (John 10:11-15)

My brothers and sisters, if anyone among you wanders from the truth and is brought back by another, you should know that whoever brings back a sinner from wandering will save the sinner's soul from death and will cover a multitude of sins. (James 5:19-20)

▶ In the Spotlight
Joy in Heaven—and in My Heart

My husband and I were married when I was seventeen years old and pregnant. Seven years and two babies later we were struggling painfully in our marriage. In my weakness I turned to my best friend's husband for attention. This led to a brief affair that devastated our families. It seemed everyone in our small town found out about what I had done.

My husband and I decided to stay together to try to work out our problems. We got counseling, and I returned to the church after many years of being away. My intentions were good but my guilt was great. I used to sit in the back of church at Sunday Mass and imagine what the people there were thinking—or would think if they knew of my sin.

One Sunday the gospel recounted the parable of the lost sheep. "I tell you," it concludes, "there will likewise be more joy in heaven over one repentant sinner than over ninety-nine righteous people who have no need to repent" (Luke 15:7). As I heard these words, I was flooded with relief and an incredible sense of hope.

This began a wonderful journey toward emotional and spiritual healing. It led me into a personal love relationship with Jesus my Lord that grows with every passing day. My husband has since come to know the Lord, and our marriage has been made new in Christ. He uses us now to minister and give hope to people in troubled marriages. The Lord has even restored my relationship with the friend with whose husband I committed adultery. Our God is truly a God of miracles!
—**Terrie Belleci,** *God's Word Today*

Act!

"All we like sheep have gone astray; we have all turned to our own way" (Isaiah 53:6).

The Sacrament of Reconciliation is also "called the *sacrament of conversion* because it makes sacramentally present Jesus' call to conversion, the first step in returning to the Father from whom one has strayed by sin" (*Catechism of the Catholic Church*, 1423).

Go to confession this week, and rejoice in receiving forgiveness for your sins. To prepare for this sacrament, ask the Holy Spirit to guide you in making a good examination of conscience.

▶ In the Spotlight
Keeping Count of My Flock

During my own years as a keeper of sheep, perhaps some of the most poignant memories are wrapped around the commingled anxiety of keeping count of my flock and repeatedly saving and restoring cast (fallen down, unable to get back up) sheep. . . . Often I would go out early and merely cast my eye across the sky. If I saw the black-winged buzzards circling overhead in their long slow spirals, anxiety would grip me. Leaving everything else I would immediately go out into the rough wild pastures and count the flock to make sure everyone was well and fit and able to be on its feet.

This is part of the pageantry and drama depicted for us in the magnificent story of the ninety and nine sheep with one astray. There is the Shepherd's deep concern; his agonizing search; his longing to find the missing one; his delight in restoring it not only to its feet but also to the flock as well as to himself.

Again and again I would spend hours searching for a single sheep that was missing. Then more often than not, I would see it at a distance, down on its back, lying helpless. At once I would start to run toward it—hurrying as fast as I could—for every minute was critical. Within me there was mingled sense of fear and joy: fear it might be too late; joy that it was found at all.

As soon as I reached the cast ewe my very first impulse was to pick it up. . . .

One of the great revelations of the heart of God given to us by Christ is that of Himself as our Shepherd. He has come to the same identical sensations of anxiety, concern and compassion for cast men and women as I had for cast sheep. This is precisely why He looked on people with such pathos and compassion. It explains His magnanimous dealing with down-and-out individuals for whom even human society had no use. It reveals why He wept over those who spurned His affection. It discloses the depth of His understanding of undone people to whom He came eagerly and quickly, ready to help, to save, to restore.

—**Phillip Keller,** *A Shepherd Looks at Psalm 23*

The Outrageous
Generosity of God

Matthew 20:1-16

1 [Jesus said to his disciples:] "For the kingdom of heaven is like a landowner who went out early in the morning to hire laborers for his vineyard. 2After agreeing with the laborers for the usual daily wage [a denarius], he sent them into his vineyard. 3When he went out about nine o'clock, he saw others standing idle in the market place; 4and he said to them, 'You also go into the vineyard, and I will pay you whatever is right.' So they went. 5When he went out again about noon and about three o'clock, he did the same. 6And about five o'clock he went out and found others standing around; and he said to them, 'Why are you standing here idle all day?' 7They said to him, 'Because no one has hired us.' He said to them, 'You also go into the vineyard.' 8When evening came, the owner of the vineyard said to his manager, 'Call the laborers and give them their pay, beginning with the last and then going to the first.' 9When those hired about five o'clock came, each of them received the usual daily wage [a denarius]. 10Now when the first came, they thought they would receive more; but each of them also received the usual daily wage. 11And when they received it, they grumbled against the landowner, 12saying, 'These last worked only one hour, and you have made them equal to us who have borne the burden of the day and the scorching heat.' 13But he replied to one of them, 'Friend, I am doing you no wrong; did you not agree with me for the usual daily wage? 14Take what belongs to you and go; I choose to give to this last the same as I give to you. 15Am I not allowed to do what I choose with what belongs to me? Or are you envious because I am generous?' 16So the last will be first, and the first will be last."

> The parable challenges the attitude and behavior of the listeners. The question is addressed to them: are you jealous because I am good for your neighbors? This question challenges them to allow such a God into their life.
> —Jan Lambrecht, SJ, *Out of the Treasure: The Parables in the Gospel of Matthew*

I choose to give to this last the same as I give to you" (Matthew 20:14). How we react to the way the landholder paid the men he hired to work in his vineyard depends on the state of our own hearts. We could respond, "Oh, what a generous employer!" or we could say, "Isn't that terribly unfair?"

In giving so liberally to those who had worked only a short time, the landowner was taking nothing away from the laborers who had worked all day. "I am doing you no wrong," he reminded those who felt cheated. "Did you not agree with me for the usual daily wage?" (Matthew 20:13). Then he got at the heart of the problem by asking the grumblers, "Are you envious because I am generous?" (20:15).

As he so often did during his public ministry, Jesus once again turned customary rules and expectations upside down. He was not concerned here with labor relations or market-based economics. Rather, with this story and its surprising twist, Jesus exposed the canker of envy in the human heart and vividly illustrated the mercy and generosity of God—generosity so unstinting that it confounds not only our logic but also our sense of justice.

As long as we insist on equating "fairness" with "equality," God's generosity will never make sense to us. We need to get past our human tendency to interpret another's gain as our loss before we can truly appreciate the magnificence of God's gift to each of us. The fact is, no matter how long we work or how hard we try, we can never *earn* God's love or his salvation through our own efforts. God freely loves us. He is eager to welcome all of us into his kingdom—sinners and latecomers as well as the upstanding and hardworking. Unreasonable? Outrageous? That's the extravagant nature of divine mercy.

In its setting in Matthew's gospel, the parable is addressed to Jesus' disciples who had left everything behind to follow him (Matthew

19:27-30). Perhaps Jesus wanted his closest companions to know that despite their sacrifice, they were not to think they merited a greater reward than others who would later follow him. If Jesus also told this parable to the crowds that flocked to listen to him, he may have been warning self-righteous scribes and Pharisees not to resent the favor he shows to sinners—a warning that we, too, should take to heart.

Since Matthew addressed his gospel most particularly to the Jewish Christians of the early church, we might further recognize in this parable an admonition to them, "God's chosen people." The gentiles, who had not labored under the strict Mosaic code for centuries, were the late-comers, yet they were receiving the same blessing of salvation as the Jewish Christians. The Jewish Christians were not to begrudge the grace freely given to the gentiles, nor were they justified in looking down on them.

No matter how long we work or how hard we try, we can never *earn* God's love or his salvation through our own efforts. God freely loves us.

Since Jesus first told this disquieting parable two thousand years ago, it has continued to speak to diverse audiences and probe the hearts of countless men and women. Today the parable of the laborers in the vineyard—perhaps better named the parable of the good employer—still challenges us with its timeless message that God freely offers to everyone who would receive it the same mercy and reward: eternal life with him. And there is no room for envy in his heavenly kingdom!

Understand!

1. The landowner merely told those hired later in the day that he would pay them "whatever is right" (Matthew 20:4). What does this seem to imply? How does this add to the suspense of the parable and increase the shock value of its ending?

_____

_____

_____

_____

_____

_____

_____

2. How did the landowner respond to the grumblers' complaints? Do you think he adequately addressed their issues? Why or why not?

_____

_____

_____

_____

_____

_____

3. Explain how you think Verse 16—"So the last will be first, and the first will be last"—relates to the rest of the parable. Note that a similar verse (Matthew 19:30) provides a link between Jesus' previous conversation with his disciples and this parable. What does Matthew's framing of the parable in this way suggest to you?

_____

_____

_____

_____

_____

_____

_____

4. How does the parable of the laborers in the vineyard act as a metaphor for the final judgment?

_____

_____

_____

_____

_____

_____

_____

5. What have you learned about human efforts and God's grace from this parable? In what ways does this parable summarize the whole message of the gospels?

_____

_____

_____

_____

_____

_____

_____

What galls those who were hired first (and us) is that there is not equal pay for equal work. It is within the frustration over this imbalance that the parable makes its point. If we insist that justice be followed to the letter, then God is not free to be merciful. If mercy, however, were taken off the table, we would all be lost. For the most essential aspects of our lives go beyond what we deserve. Are we owed life or health or love? It is only because God gives us more than what we deserve that we have happiness, salvation, and eternal life.

God is not limited by our desire to measure everything out according to our merits. God will be generous to whomever God chooses. Even though we may at times be peeved that others are recipients of God's mercy, such gifts to them are good news for us. Their God is our God. Mercy to them is an assurance that mercy will be available to us.

—**George Smiga,** *God's Word Today*

Grow!

1. In what ways does the action of the landowner reflect your concept of God and his mercy? In what ways does it differ?

_____

_____

_____

_____

_____

_____

2. How do you usually respond to the good fortune of others? If you have ever felt jealous or resentful of another person's blessing or benefit, how did you handle your feelings?

_____

_____

_____

_____

_____

_____

3. Recall a situation when you were generous or acted with mercy toward someone. How did your kindness affect this person? What motivated you to act so generously?

_____

_____

_____

_____

_____

_____

4. Several Fathers of the Church interpreted the hours of the day in the parable as an analogy for the point in life when a person responded to God's call—childhood, adolescence, midlife, the later years. Where would you place yourself in such a time framework?

_____

_____

_____

_____

_____

_____

5. How does this parable challenge your own concepts of fairness and justice? How does it move you to embrace God's idea of "fairness"?

_____

_____

_____

_____

_____

_____

▶ **In the Spotlight**
Eye of Evil, Eye of Envy

"Are you envious because I am generous?" the landowner asked the grumblers. The literal translation of the original Greek of Matthew's gospel would be, "Is your eye evil because I am good?"

This "evil eye" is the eye of envy. The Book of Sirach, which includes maxims and sayings written in Hebrew by the Jewish sage Ben Sira around 200 B.C., was later translated into Greek by the author's grandson. A passage from this Greek translation reads, "The eye of the greedy person is not satisfied with his share. . . . An evil eye is envious over bread, and it is lacking on his table" (Sirach 14:9-10). A similar expression equating the eye with greed, avarice, and envy was used again by Ben Sira in Sirach 31:13. Jesus refers to the state of the "eye" as healthy or unhealthy, calling it the lamp that brings light or darkness to the rest of the body (Matthew 6:22-23).

Reflect!

1. Reflect on these words from Pope John Paul II calling you to labor in God's vineyard:

> From that distant day the call of the Lord Jesus "You go into my vineyard too" (Matthew 20:4) never fails to resound in the course of history: It is addressed to every person who comes into this world. . . . Since the work that awaits everyone in the vineyard of the Lord is so great, there is no place for idleness.
>
> God calls me and sends me forth as a laborer in his vineyard. He calls me and sends me forth to work for the coming of his kingdom in history. This personal vocation and mission defines the dignity and the responsibility of each member of the lay faithful. (*On the Vocation and the Mission of the Lay Faithful in the Church and in the World*)

2. Reflect on the following passages to deepen your appreciation of the parable you have just studied:

> The greedy person stirs up strife,
>   but whoever trusts in the LORD will be enriched.
> (Proverbs 28:25)

> The eye of the greedy person is not satisfied with
>   his share;
>   greedy injustice withers the soul. (Sirach 14:9)

> What then are we to say? Is there injustice on God's part? By no means! For he says to Moses,
> "I will have mercy on whom I have mercy,
>   and I will have compassion on whom I have
>   compassion."

So it depends not on human will or exertion, but on God who shows mercy. . . . So then he has mercy on whomever he chooses. . . . (Romans 9:14-16, 18)

God, who is rich in mercy, out of the great love with which he loved us even when we were dead through our trespasses, made us alive together with Christ—by grace you have been saved—and raised us up with him and seated us with him in the heavenly places in Christ Jesus, so that in the ages to come he might show the immeasurable riches of his grace in kindness toward us in Christ Jesus. (Ephesians 2:4-7)

[W]hen the goodness and loving kindness of God our Savior appeared, he saved us, not because of any works of righteousness that we had done, but according to his mercy, through the water of rebirth and renewal by the Holy Spirit. This Spirit he poured out on us richly through Jesus Christ our Savior, so that, having been justified by his grace, we might become heirs according to the hope of eternal life. (Titus 3:4-7)

▶ In the Spotlight
A Denarius a Day

In the early days of human history, trade was conducted by bartering, and payment for services was made in goods. Later, precious metals such as gold and silver were used, with value measured by weight. Coinage was introduced around the seventh century B.C. The earliest coins were simply pieces of metal of a standard weight impressed with a seal. Consequently, coins were often named after the weight they represented—a shekel equaled 11.4 grams; a talent, 30 kilograms.

During the first century A.D., three different currencies were used in Palestine: the official imperial money (Roman standard); provincial money minted in Antioch and Tyre (Greek standard); and local Jewish money, most likely minted in Caesarea.

The denarius was a Roman coin made of silver. During Jesus' ministry, the denarius showed the head of Tiberius, the emperor of the Roman Empire from A.D. 17 to 37. Soldiers and farm workers were paid a denarius a day for their services or labor, which was considered the standard wage, enough to cover life's basic necessities.

Act!

Make a list of the ways you have experienced God's generosity to you. Then turn your list into your own "litany of thanksgiving," praising God and thanking him for his mercy and loving kindness.

▶ In the Spotlight
Celebrating Our Oneness

Suppose the all-day workers in the parable had walked home with the one-hour workers, rejoicing all the way over the generosity of the employer. Wouldn't that have been a beautiful time of sharing for all? If we are able to rejoice in God's grace for all, without comparisons and without envy, we live in shared joy and tender appreciation for everyone. We learn then what it means to love both neighbor and enemy. . . .

It is a rare person who loves enough to rejoice in all goodness, whether he or she benefits directly or not. Yet we can all practice this happy attitude. When we hear of something wonderful falling into another's life, we can set aside that nagging "But what about me?" and simply enjoy the beauty with that person. We may even celebrate it. It is recommended that we do this, even though in the beginning it may feel unreal, if we have habitually envied every good thing that happened to others. Our emotions carry on in their habits, but do our emotions tell us the truth? Rarely! . . .

Let's not count the hours we work, nor the hours another works. Let us press on, our eyes on the goal and our hands joined for the going. God awaits his full entry into our hearts.

—**Marilyn Gustin,** *How to Read and Pray the Parables*

Joyfully Discovering the Kingdom

The pearl of great price and the treasure hidden in a field were a reminder of the vastness of what is at stake. Compared with that, all other successes are meaningless; men will make the kingdom their own only if they are willing to sacrifice everything else for it.
—**Frank Sheed,** *To Know Christ Jesus*

Matthew 13:44-46

⁴⁴ [Jesus said to his disciples:] "The kingdom of heaven is like treasure hidden in a field, which someone found and hid; then in his joy he goes and sells all that he has and buys that field.

⁴⁵ "Again, the kingdom of heaven is like a merchant in search of fine pearls; ⁴⁶on finding one pearl of great value, he went and sold all that he had and bought it."

J esus had just dismissed the crowds after telling them the parable of the weeds and the wheat. The disciples followed him into a house, asking for an explanation. He provided one (Matthew 13:36-43)—and then promptly told them several more parables about the kingdom of God, including this pair about the hidden treasure and the pearl. Did the disciples see their own experiences mirrored in these twin parables?

The man who discovered the buried treasure sold everything he possessed—perhaps a donkey, his wife's weaving loom, his family's house and furniture—to acquire it. The merchant, too, sold all he had to buy the exquisite pearl that far surpassed any he had ever seen before. Each man's response to his discovery was the same: Recognizing his find to be of inestimable worth, he sacrificed whatever was necessary to make it his own. The purchasers didn't haggle over price. Nor did they bemoan what their acquisitions would cost them. On the contrary, they made their transactions joyfully, because what both men stood to gain was so tremendous that it made any monetary cost, any sacrifice, any leap of faith insignificant in comparison.

Perhaps like the man who unexpectedly stumbled on the fortune hidden in the ground, the disciples hadn't been actively looking for the Messiah. Or they may have been more like the merchant, seeking something of great intrinsic worth that would enrich their lives. No matter whether they had come upon their treasure inadvertently or had found it after a long search, the disciples had responded like the men in the parable.

The disciples had given up everything that previously defined their lives—their livelihoods, their homes, and their families—to follow an itinerant rabbi who they believed to be the long-awaited Messiah (Mark 1:16-20). Following Jesus required total surrender and commitment (Matthew 16:24-26; Luke 9:23, 14:26-33). It also required an unwavering faith that the kingdom Jesus was inaugurating was truly the "pearl of great price." Through this pair of parables, Jesus reassured them that, yes, what they had given up could not even begin to compare with what he would give them in return. "Truly I tell you, there is no one who has left house or wife or brothers or parents or children, for the sake of the kingdom of God, who will not get back very much more in this age, and in the age to come eternal life" (Luke 18:29-30).

The message of these brief parables offers encouragement to us as well. It's not easy to make a radical investment of ourselves in Christ. It requires an act of faith to live singleheartedly for him. We may find ourselves at different stages in our journey—perhaps reluctant to sacrifice certain things in our lives, perhaps giving up something for a time only to take it back. But there is literally everything to gain by persevering. And as we come to joyfully recognize "the surpassing worth of knowing Christ Jesus" (Philippians 3:8), we become more like the men in the parables—rushing off to "sell" all we have for the great treasure of Jesus reigning in our lives.

> Through this pair of parables, Jesus reassured them that, yes, what they had given up could not even begin to compare with what he would give them in return.

Understand!

1. What might it have cost the two men—besides money—to possess what they had discovered? What risks might have been involved in making their purchases?

_____

_____

_____

_____

_____

_____

2. Why do you think Jesus used hidden treasure and a pearl to describe the kingdom of heaven? What clues do these parables provide about the nature of God's kingdom?

_____

_____

_____

_____

_____

_____

3. Jesus notes that the man in the field experienced joy even as he prepared to sell all of his possessions to buy the plot of land. How does this further emphasize Jesus' point about the value of the kingdom of heaven? About the value of worldly things?

_____

_____

_____

_____

_____

_____

_____

4. Jesus told these parables to his disciples in private, not to the crowds in general (Matthew 13:36). What does this suggest to you? What light does this shed on the meaning and cost of discipleship?

_____

_____

_____

_____

_____

_____

5. Matthew's gospel places the parables about the treasure and the pearl between Jesus' explanation of the parable of the weeds among the wheat and a similar parable about a net thrown into the sea, from which the good fish are separated from the bad. Why do you think Matthew put the parables in that order?

_____

_____

_____

_____

_____

_____

_____

▶ In the Spotlight
Wisdom from the Church Fathers

By the pearl of price is to be understood the sweetness of the heavenly kingdom, which, he that has found it, sells all and buys. For he that, as far as is permitted, has had perfect knowledge of the sweetness of the heavenly life, readily leaves all things that he has loved on earth; all that once pleased him among earthly possessions now appears to have lost its beauty, for the splendor of that precious pearl is alone seen in his mind.
—**St. Gregory the Great**, *Homilies on the Gospels*

Christ is the treasure which was hid in the field, that is, in this world (for "the field is the world"); but the treasure hid in the Scriptures is Christ, since he was pointed out by means of types and parables. . . . It [the Old Testament law and prophecies] is a treasure, hid indeed in a field, but brought to light by the cross of Christ.
—**St. Irenaeus**, *Against Heresies*

A man seeking goodly pearls has found one pearl of great price; that is, he who is seeking good men with whom he may live profitably, finds one alone, Christ Jesus, without sin.
—**St. Augustine**, *Quaest. in Matt.*

Grow!

1. Was your own "discovery" of Christ seemingly accidental and unexpected or the result of much searching on your part? How did you respond to this discovery?

_____

_____

_____

_____

_____

_____

_____

_____

2. What has your decision to follow Christ cost you? What part of the "purchase price" to obtain the treasure did you find most difficult to pay? Are you withholding any part of the price? If so, why?

_____

_____

_____

_____

_____

_____

_____

_____

3. Which aspect of the parable speaks to you most personally right now? The joy of discovery? The value of the kingdom? The total commitment of self to God? Why?

_____

_____

_____

_____

_____

_____

_____

_____

4. In what ways have you shared the treasure you've found in Christ with others? In what ways could you share that treasure even more?

_____

_____

_____

_____

_____

_____

5. How does the way you use your resources—your talents, time, money—reflect the value you place on God's kingdom?

_____

_____

_____

_____

_____

_____

▶ In the Spotlight
Contemporary Voices

The traditional interpretation sees the farmer and the merchant as disciples or would-be disciples. But it is possible that both are images of God himself, who has given what is most precious to him, his own Son (see Matthew 21:37), to purchase (= redeem) his people. Perhaps it is only when the human person realizes the extent of God's extravagance that he can respond with similar totality.

—**George Montague, SM,** *Companion God: A Cross-Cultural Commentary on the Gospel of Matthew*

The gospel parables of the treasure and the pearl of great price, for which one sells all one's possessions, are eloquent and effective images of the radical and unconditional nature of the decision demanded by the kingdom of God. The radical nature of the decision to follow Jesus is admirably expressed in his own words: "Whoever would save his life will lose it; and whoever loses his life for my sake and the gospel's will save it" (Mark 8:35).

—**Pope John Paul II,** *The Splendor of Truth*

Reflect!

1. Making Jesus and the kingdom of heaven our greatest treasure affects the other priorities and goals in our lives. Consider what adjustments you might need to make to better reflect the value you place on Jesus and building his kingdom.

2. Reflect on the following passages to enhance your understanding of the parables you have just studied:

[T]he price of wisdom is above pearls. (Job 28:18)

If you seek [wisdom] like silver,
   and search for it as for hidden treasures—
then you will understand the fear of the LORD
   and find the knowledge of God. (Proverbs 2:4-5)

Jesus said to [the rich young man], "If you wish to be perfect, go, sell your possessions, and give the money to the poor, and you will have treasure in heaven; then come, follow me." When the young man heard this word, he went away grieving, for he had many possessions.
(Matthew 19:21-22)

[Jesus] said to his disciples, "Do not be afraid, little flock, for it is your Father's good pleasure to give you the kingdom. Sell your possessions, and give alms. Make purses for yourselves that do not wear out, an unfailing treasure in heaven, where no thief comes near and no moth destroys. For where your treasure is, there your heart will be also." (Luke 12:32-34)

Yet whatever gains I had, these I have come to regard as loss because of Christ. More than that, I regard everything as loss because of the surpassing value of knowing Christ Jesus my Lord. For his sake I have suffered the loss of all things, and I regard them as rubbish, in order that I may gain Christ and be found in him. (Philippians 3:7-9)

▶ In the Spotlight
Pearls Most Precious

With their beautiful luster and glowing iridescence, pearls were considered to have far greater value than gold in the ancient world. A fragment of the oldest known pearl jewelry was found in the sarcophagus of a Persian princess who died in 520 B.C. Egyptians prized pearls so much that they, too, were buried with them. In the first century B.C., Julius Caesar decreed that only rulers of the Roman Empire could wear pearls, the ultimate symbol of wealth and social stature. Cleopatra reportedly dropped a pearl into a glass of wine and then drank it, simply to win a wager with Mark Antony that she could consume the wealth of an entire nation in a single meal. In A.D. 77, Pliny the Elder observed in his *Natural History* that pearls were "the richest merchandise of all, and the most sovereign commodity throughout the whole world."

Pearls are formed in the depths of the sea by oysters, mussels, and mollusks. Merchants in Jesus' day went to the Red Sea, the Persian Gulf, and the Indian Ocean in search of pearls of the highest quality. *Unios*, the Latin word used to describe a large, fine pearl, literally means "unique" or "singular," since no two of these natural wonders are exactly alike.

Act!

This week share about the treasure you've found in Christ and the joy of this discovery with at least one person with whom you have never discussed your faith.

▶ In the Spotlight
What a Treasure!

Those two parables of Jesus catch the imagination. We can picture a poor farm laborer working in the field, working with a hoe or something like that, and by accident, just beneath the surface he hits something hard, uncovers it, and it's a wooden box with a great treasure in it.

The other parable involves not a poor man, but a well-to-do merchant who travels to faraway places. One day he sees a pile of so-so pearls and suddenly, in amongst them is a pearl that looks like the rest, but his practiced eye can see that it is a magnificent pearl worth a fortune.

Jesus didn't tell these fascinating stories just to entertain his audience. What is Jesus teaching us?

Remember, in both cases the valuable discovery was right there in front of everyone else. The treasure was just beneath the surface of a field that people passed by or walked through all the time. The pearl was in open sight, on a table with all the other pearls. It's just that nobody noticed.

Here's what I want you to do. Take just a few seconds now and look ahead to the things coming up in your life this week. It doesn't have to be something special—just the regular stuff of the week. Take 20 seconds to think about your schedule this week.

[20-second pause]

Okay. Now, the panorama of the week in your mind right now . . . just beneath the surface of everything in it, and mixed together with everything that's part of it, is a great treasure. It is God. Imagine. God mixed in with all that. God is in all this week's stuff, present, active, part of it, with you, helping you, asking you simply to do your best to bring some goodness to it.

What a treasure! To have God there. Especially in some of the things that aren't entirely pleasant, or are boring. What a treasure to have God there. . . . God is with us in everything, and it's especially difficult to notice God's presence in the not-so-good parts of our lives, or in the regular, routine parts of our lives. But God is there, even though God's presence can go unnoticed—just like no one noticed the treasure in that field, or that magnificent pearl in that pile of pearls.

—**Bishop Kenneth Untener,** *Homily*

"You Can't Take It with You"

Luke 12:13-21

13 Someone in the crowd said to him, "Teacher, tell my brother to divide the family inheritance with me." 14But he said to him, "Friend, who set me to be a judge or arbitrator over you?" 15And he said to them, "Take care! Be on your guard against all kinds of greed, for one's life does not consist in the abundance of possessions." 16Then he told them a parable: "The land of a rich man produced abundantly. 17And he thought to himself, 'What should I do, for I have no place to store my crops?' 18Then he said, 'I will do this: I will pull down my barns and build larger ones, and there I will store all my grain and my goods. 19And I will say to my soul, Soul, you have ample goods laid up for many years; relax, eat, drink, be merry.' 20But God said to him, 'You fool! This very night your life is being demanded of you. And the things you have prepared, whose will they be?' 21So it is with those who store up treasures for themselves but are not rich toward God."

The parable . . . shows the pointlessness of greed. Possessions, even an abundance of possessions, cannot give us security; they can only give us an illusion of security. And that illusion can distract us from the true source of our security, God's care for us. The folly of the rich farmer lay not in his having full barns, but in his believing that his full barns were all he needed.

—**George Martin**, *God's Word Today*

The request that prompted Jesus to tell this parable might seem to be a rather innocent one. Someone in the crowd just wanted to receive his fair share of his family's possessions. But to Jesus, the man's concern with money betrayed the fact that he had missed the point—he had focused his attention on the things of this world rather than storing up treasures in the kingdom of God.

So Jesus distanced himself from this man's personal concerns and proceeded to tell a story about a man with so much earthly wealth that he thought his future was secured. The rich landowner had "ample goods for many years," so why not "relax, eat, drink, [and] be merry"? It's easy to imagine this man at his leisure, enjoying the fruits of his labors.

So why is this man a fool? Don't we all take measures to provide for our future security? The problem with the man in the parable is that he didn't have his priorities straight. The wealthy man put all his trust in his possessions instead of putting his trust in God. He sought happiness and security by stockpiling his wealth, not even thinking of sharing it with others. We know from his monologue that he was self-centered—the personal pronoun "I" appears six times and the possessive pronoun "my" five times—so the possibility of sharing his abundance with others apparently never even crossed his mind. He didn't thank God for his prosperity, nor did he seek advice from anyone about how to put his surplus to good use. His only thought was to build a bigger barn in which to store his wealth for his own future. He was so preoccupied with his possessions that he idolized them, letting them usurp God's rightful place in his life.

Suddenly, when the man was confronted with his imminent death, the senselessness of his actions was made plain to him. God himself says: "You fool! This very night your life is being demanded of you. And the things you have prepared, whose will they be?" (Luke 12:20).

The wealthy landowner's actions and his perspective on life were based on a set of falsehoods—which is why he was called a fool. How easy it is to deceive ourselves just as this rich fool did. We're susceptible to the same all-too-human tendencies that he was, and our vision can be just as short sighted and distorted. We try to control our own destinies, when it is God who has ultimate control. Perhaps we base our security in riches and things we can see, forgetting that we can only be secure in God. Or, focused on our own well-being and interests, we neglect the needs of our neighbor. We forget that all we have comes from God—it's not really ours. We mistakenly live for the present, giving no thought to securing our eternal future.

The parable of the rich fool is another of Jesus' pointed and disquieting reminders that we are not to invest ourselves in the perishable riches of earth, but rather in the enduring riches of heaven, that will gain us eternal interest (Luke 12:21, 33). When we perceive the truth about God and the fullness of life that he offers us, we'll be eager to be "rich toward God" (12:21). "For where [our] treasure is, there [our] heart will be also" (Matthew 6:21; Luke 12:34).

> We try to control our own destinies, when it is God who has ultimate control. Perhaps we base our security in riches and things we can see, forgetting that we can only be secure in God.

Understand!

1. Why do you think Jesus refused to judge the dispute between two brothers about their inheritance? What does the parable indicate about how God judges people like these brothers?

_____

_____

_____

_____

_____

_____

2. Jesus said, "One's life does not consist in the abundance of possessions" (Luke 12:15). According to his parable, in what should our life consist?

_____

_____

_____

_____

_____

3. The Old Testament describes a fool as one who lives as though God does not exist (Psalm 14:1; 53:1). In what ways did the rich man forget about God or act like he did not exist?

_____

_____

_____

_____

_____

_____

_____

4. In concrete terms, what do you think it means to "store up treasures" for ourselves (Luke 12:21)? To be "rich toward God"?

_____

_____

_____

_____

_____

_____

_____

5. According to Jesus' words in Luke 12:22-34, which immediately follow this parable, we should trust in our heavenly Father to meet our material needs. How does his teaching build on the message of the parable?

_____

_____

_____

_____

_____

_____

_____

▶ In the Spotlight
From the *Catechism of the Catholic Church*

Love for the poor is incompatible with immoderate love of riches or their selfish use. (2445)

The tenth commandment ["You shall not covet . . . anything that is your neighbor's"] forbids *greed* and the desire to amass earthly goods without limit. It forbids *avarice* arising from a passion for riches and their attendant power. (2536)

The Lord grieves over the rich, because they find their consolation in the abundance of goods. (2547)

Desire for true happiness frees man from his immoderate attachment to the goods of this world so that he can find his fulfillment in the vision and beatitude of God. (2548)

Grow!

1. What forms of greed do you recognize in your life? Desire to acquire things for their own sake? Selfish attachment to your possessions? Hoarding? How can you guard against such attitudes and practices?

_____

_____

_____

_____

_____

_____

_____

2. If you find yourself at times basing your security on material goods, income, or achievements, why do you think this is the case? What would help you trust less in worldly things and more in God?

_____

_____

_____

_____

_____

_____

_____

3. In what ways does a preoccupation with satisfying our material needs keep us from serving God and his people? What might help you increase your focus on the values of God's kingdom and on eternal life?

_____

_____

_____

_____

_____

_____

_____

4. Make a list of the qualities you think are necessary to be a good and prudent steward of God's gifts. Which of those qualities would you like to grow in?

_____

_____

_____

_____

_____

_____

_____

5. What have you learned about God and what is important to him from this parable? About yourself and what is important to you?

_____

_____

_____

_____

_____

_____

▶ In the Spotlight
Contemporary Voices

Neither individuals nor nations should regard the possession of more and more goods as the ultimate objective. Every kind of progress is a two-edged sword. It is necessary if man is to grow as a human being; yet it can also enslave him, if he comes to regard it as the supreme good and cannot look beyond it. When this happens, men harden their hearts, shut out others from their minds, and gather together solely for reasons of self-interest rather than out of friendship; dissension and disunity follow soon after.

Thus the exclusive pursuit of material possessions prevents man's growth as a human being and stands in opposition to his true grandeur. Avarice, in individuals and in nations, is the most obvious form of stultified moral development.
—**Pope Paul VI,** _On the Development of Peoples_

Reflect!

1. Still yourself and quietly meditate a while on the inevitability of your death. In this light, are there any ways that you should change how you relate to status, possessions, and material goods?

2. Reflect on the following passages to deepen your insight into the parable you have just studied:

> [Job] said: "Naked I came from my mother's womb, and naked shall I return there; the LORD gave, and the LORD has taken away; blessed be the name of the LORD." (Job 1:21)

> All day long the wicked covet,
>   but the righteous give and do not hold back.
> (Proverbs 21:26)

> Set your minds on things that are above, not on things that are on earth, for you have died, and your life is hidden with Christ in God. When Christ who is your life is revealed, then you also will be revealed with him in glory. Put to death, therefore, whatever in you is earthly: fornication, impurity, passion, evil desire, and greed (which is idolatry).
> (Colossians 3:2-5)

> There is great gain in godliness combined with contentment; for we brought nothing into the world, so that we can take nothing out of it; but if we have food and clothing, we will be content with these. But those who want to be rich fall into temptation and are trapped by many senseless and harmful desires that plunge people into ruin and destruction. For the love of money is a root of all kinds of evil, and in their eagerness to be rich some have

wandered away from the faith and pierced themselves with many pains. (1 Timothy 6:6-10)

As for those who in the present age are rich, command them not to be haughty, or to set their hopes on the uncertainty of riches, but rather on God who richly provides us with everything for our enjoyment. They are to do good, to be rich in good works, generous, and ready to share, thus storing up for themselves the treasure of a good foundation for the future, so that they may take hold of the life that really is life. (1 Timothy 6:17-19)

▶ In the Spotlight
The Insatiable Desire for More

Pleonexia is the Greek word for "greediness" or "covetousness." It carries overtones of an insatiable desire for more and more. The verb form is commonly used to describe the actions of those who try to take advantage of others or strive ambitiously for gain, and the adjective is descriptive of one who never has enough.

Jesus named *pleonexia*, or avarice, one of the evils that come from within the heart and defile a person (Mark 7:21-23). St. Paul included it among the characteristics of the ungodly and wicked (Romans 1:29) and of those who are alienated from God by their hardness of heart (Ephesians 4:19).

As Christians who have been buried with Christ in baptism and raised up with him, we are to "put to death" in ourselves "whatever is earthly: fornication, impurity, passion, evil desire, and greed—*pleonexia*—(which is idolatry)" (Colossians 3:5).

Act!

Simplify your life! Are you "storing up" things unnecessarily? Take some time this week to begin to sort through your clothing, household goods, and other possessions. Donate what you don't need or aren't making use of to a charitable organization so that others will be able to benefit from these items.

If this is a big step for you to take, begin slowly and ask God to guide you.

▶ In the Spotlight
Gifts of Love

In Calcutta, we didn't have sugar; and a little Hindu child, four years old, he heard Mother Teresa has no sugar. And he went home and he told his parents: "I will not eat sugar for three days. I will give my sugar to Mother Teresa." After three days, the parents brought the child to our house. In his hand he had a little bottle of sugar . . . the sugar of a little child. He could scarcely pronounce my name, but he knew he loved a great love because he loved until it hurt. It hurt him to give up sugar for three days. But that little child taught me that to be able to love a great love, it is not how much we give but how much loving is put in the giving.

—**Blessed Mother Teresa of Calcutta**, *Respect Life . . . In the Words of Mother Teresa of Calcutta*

Sometime back two young people came to our house and they gave me lots, lots of money. And I said, "Where, where did you get so much money?" And they said, "Two days ago we got married, and before marriage we decided we will buy no wedding clothes, we will have no wedding feast. We will give you the money." For a Hindu family that's a big, big, big sacrifice because wedding day is one of the biggest days in their life. And again I offered, "Why, why did you do that?" And they said, "We love each other so much that we wanted to share the joy of loving with the people you serve, and we experience the joy of loving."

—**Blessed Mother Teresa of Calcutta,** *Love: A Fruit Always in Season*

"Be Merciful to Me, O God"

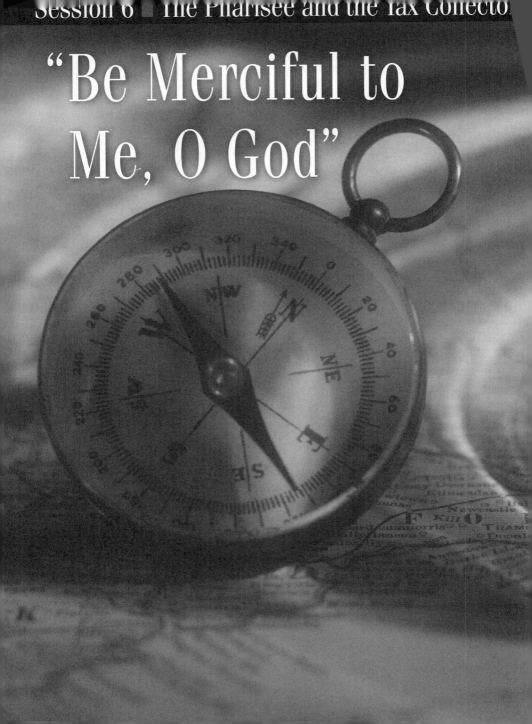

Luke 18:9-14

[9] [Jesus] also told this parable to some who trusted in themselves that they were righteous and regarded others with contempt: [10]"Two men went up to the temple to pray, one a Pharisee and the other a tax collector. [11]The Pharisee, standing by himself, was praying thus, 'God, I thank you that I am not like other people: thieves, rogues, adulterers, or even like this tax collector. [12]I fast twice a week; I give a tenth of all my income.' [13]But the tax collector, standing far off, would not even look up to heaven, but was beating his breast and saying, 'God, be merciful to me, a sinner!' [14]I tell you, this man went down to his home justified rather than the other; for all who exalt themselves will be humbled, but all who humble themselves will be exalted."

The Pharisee was not rejoicing so much in his own clean bill of health as in comparing it with the diseases of others. He came to the doctor. It would have been more worthwhile to inform him by confession of the things that were wrong with himself instead of keeping his wounds secret and having the nerve to crow over the scars of others. It is not surprising that the tax collector went away cured, since he had not been ashamed of showing where he felt pain.

—St. Augustine, *Sermon 351.1*

With the parable of the Pharisee and the tax collector, Jesus once again took his listeners by surprise. His Jewish contemporaries would have esteemed the Pharisee as a model of religious propriety, concurred with the man's high opinion of himself, and assumed that he deserved God's favor. They also would have looked down on the tax collector and scorned him. Yet, in another unsettling reversal of roles and expectations, Jesus commended not the "saint" but the "sinner."

Jesus' story made clear that this pious and devout Pharisee not only followed the law but even went beyond it. Jews were required to fast only one day each year, on the Day of Atonement; he fasted twice each week. Likewise, Jews tithed on their produce (Deuteronomy 14:22), whereas he tithed on his entire income. Glorying in his good works, the Pharisee confessed no sin or fault before God, because he was blind to any. He saw only the sins of others.

Local tax collectors were considered ritually unclean by their fellow Jews since they were employed by the Roman forces occupying Palestine and associated with gentiles. They were further despised as corrupt scoundrels because they often defrauded their own countrymen. Jesus' listeners would have been appalled that such a man dared even to enter the temple, God's holy dwelling place. The tax collector knew he did not measure up to the law and didn't claim to be good or holy. Yet what was lacking in the Pharisee's prayer—recognition of his need for God and repentance—made up the whole of the tax collector's plea.

Humility is the recognition of the truth of who we are in relation to God. It is the ability to see clearly that God is our creator and the source of all life and goodness. Without him, we are nothing and have nothing. The tax collector had no illusions about himself or about God. He could see that by his actions he had failed to please God and that he was greatly in need of God's mercy. The Pharisee, however, was harboring two illusions—one, that he had no sin, and the other, that his religious acts alone earned him God's favor. His greatest sin was pride. He trusted in himself rather than trusting in God.

When we fail to recognize our need for God, we also fail to recognize our need to pray. Whatever the tax collector's sins, it was his disposition of humility, his recognition of the truth, and his desire for forgiveness that "justified" him. He received God's mercy not because he deserved it or even because he thought he did, but because he asked for it through humble prayer.

> Whatever the tax collector's sins, it was his disposition of humility, his recognition of the truth, and his desire for forgiveness that "justified" him.

Jesus told this parable to "some who trusted in themselves that they were righteous and regarded others with contempt" (Luke 18:9). Its message was not directed to Jesus' first-century hearers alone. As we look into the mirror of God's word, may we have the humility to see ourselves as we truly are—and the grace to see the Lord as he truly is. For our God is merciful and compassionate, always willing and eager to "justify" each and every one of us when we come to him with repentant hearts.

Understand!

1. What adjectives would you use to describe the Pharisee? What positive traits do you see in his actions and character? What flaws?

_____

_____

_____

_____

_____

_____

2. What does the Pharisee's prayer reveal about his image and concept of God? In your opinion, what was the point of his prayer?

_____

_____

_____

_____

_____

_____

3. Compare and contrast the tax collector's way of approaching God with the Pharisee's. Pay attention not only to the two men's words, but also to their gestures and posture.

_____

_____

_____

_____

_____

_____

4. How would you characterize the tax collector's attitude toward God? His attitude toward himself?

_____

_____

_____

_____

_____

_____

5. How do you think Jesus' hearers reacted to this parable? What reasons can you offer for your answer?

_____

_____

_____

_____

_____

▶ In the Spotlight
Contemporary Voices

The Pharisee does not receive God's free gift of justification because he sees no need of it. He has justified himself. He confuses goodness (which he possessed) with perfection (which he did not). This is a common failing in religious people. Instead of looking *up*, at the all-holy God, the Pharisee looks *around*, at others. Discerning, rightly, that others have not achieved his level of goodness, he looks *down* on his fellow worshiper in the temple who, aware of how unworthy he is to stand in that sacred place, stands far off with bowed head, beating his breast in a gesture of humility as he pleads with God for mercy and forgiveness.

To compare ourselves with others is always a mistake. Such comparisons lead either to discouragement, when we find that others are better than we are; or to complacency, when we see that they are worse. Comparing ourselves with others is mistaken, too, because we do not know, and can never know, the difficulties against which others must contend. If I had been dealt the hand of the sister or brother who seems to have done so badly in life, can I be confident that I might not have done even worse?

—**John Jay Hughes,** *Stories Jesus Told: Modern Meditations on the Parables*

Grow!

1. What has this parable shown you about your image of God? Does your understanding of God or your attitude toward him need to be corrected in any way?

_____

_____

_____

_____

_____

2. In what ways has this parable challenged or changed your way of thinking about yourself? About the value you place on your efforts to please God?

_____

_____

_____

_____

_____

_____

3. Do you feel comfortable identifying yourself with the tax collector? Why or why not? What have you learned from him and from his prayer?

_____

_____

_____

_____

_____

_____

4. How easily do you fall into the trap of comparing your good deeds or your practice of the faith with the actions of others? Why? How can you avoid this pitfall?

_____

_____

_____

_____

_____

5. By looking at the Pharisee, do you recognize any ways in which you've been blind to your own failings? If so, write a prayer to Jesus asking him to forgive you and to help you change.

_____

_____

_____

_____

_____

_____

▶ In the Spotlight
From the *Catechism of the Catholic Church*

[W]hen we pray, do we speak from the height of our pride and will, or "out of the depths" of a humble and contrite heart? He who humbles himself will be exalted; *humility* is the foundation of prayer. Only when we humbly acknowledge that "we do not know how to pray as we ought," are we ready to receive freely the gift of prayer. (2559)

[The parable of] "the Pharisee and the tax collector," concerns the *humility* of the heart that prays, "God, be merciful to me a sinner!" The Church continues to make this prayer its own: *Kyrie eleison!* (2613)

Reflect!

1. Reflect on the gestures and postures you use when you pray. Perhaps you genuflect, bow your head, kneel, or lift up your hands. These outward physical actions are meant to be an expression of the inward disposition of the heart.

   When you perform such actions, are you conscious of their meaning? How might you use such actions more effectively in the way you relate to God?

2. Reflect on the following passages to enrich your understanding of the parable you have just studied:

   > Have mercy on me, O God,
   >   according to your steadfast love;
   > according to your abundant mercy

blot out my transgressions.
Wash me thoroughly from my iniquity,
  and cleanse me from my sin.
For I know my transgressions,
  and my sin is ever before me. . . .
Purge me with hyssop, and I shall be clean;
  wash me, and I shall be whiter than snow.
(Psalm 51:1-3, 7)

For though the LORD is high, he regards the lowly;
  but the haughty he perceives from far away.
(Psalm 138:6)

For thus says the high and lofty one
  who inhabits eternity, whose name is Holy:
I dwell in the high and holy place,
    and also with those who are contrite and humble
      in spirit,
  to revive the spirit of the humble,
    and to revive the heart of the contrite.
(Isaiah 57:15)

[Jesus said:] "Do not judge, so that you may not be judged. For with the judgment you make you will be judged, and the measure you give will be the measure you get. Why do you see the speck in your neighbor's eye, but do not notice the log in your own eye?" (Matthew 7:1, 3)

Humble yourselves therefore under the mighty hand of God, so that he may exalt you in due time. (1 Peter 5:6)

▶ In the Spotlight
The Jesus Prayer

For centuries, Christians across the world have invoked the name of the Lord in the "Jesus Prayer," which is expressed most commonly as "Lord Jesus Christ, Son of God, have mercy on us sinners." The prayer finds it origins in St. Paul's beautiful hymn about Jesus' sacrifice for our sins, which ends,

> so that at the name of Jesus
>> every knee should bend
>> in heaven and on earth and under the earth,
> and every tongue should confess
>> that Jesus Christ is Lord,
>> to the glory of God the Father. (Philippians 2:6-11)

The Jesus Prayer incorporates, as well, the humble entreaty of the tax collector in the parable and the cry of the blind men who begged Jesus for their sight. Indeed, the Jesus Prayer is so powerful that "[b]y it the heart is opened to human wretchedness and the Savior's mercy" (*Catechism of the Catholic Church*, 2667).

With the words of the Jesus Prayer, we make a perfect profession of faith, for it sums up the essentials of what we know and believe about the Lord. As we pray these few simple words, we confess our own sinfulness, cry out for God's mercy, and open ourselves to his forgiveness and his healing presence in our lives. Busy as we are with our families, our work, and our daily responsibilities, we can enter more deeply into a life of continual prayer by repeating the Jesus Prayer frequently throughout the day.

Act!

"Lord Jesus Christ, Son of God, have mercy on me, a sinner!"

Pray the Jesus Prayer as often as you can this week—while you are driving, doing household chores, taking a quiet pause in the day, jogging—whenever it comes to mind. Let the words of this prayer sink deep into your heart and remind you that you are always in the presence of God, no matter what you are doing.

▶ In the Spotlight
Wisdom from the Church Fathers

The one guilty of insolent behavior suffered the loss of his justice and forfeited his reward by his bold self-reliance. He was judged inferior to a humble man and a sinner because in his self-exaltation he did not await the judgment of God but pronounced it himself. Never place yourself above anyone, not even great sinners. Humility often saves a sinner who has committed many terrible transgressions.
—**St. Basil the Great,** *On Humility*

In the case of that Pharisee who was praying, the things he said were true. Since he was saying them out of pride and the tax collector was telling his sins with humility, the confession of sins of the last was more pleasing to God than the acknowledgment of the almsgiving of the first. It is more difficult to confess one's sins than one's righteousness. God looks on the one who carries a heavy burden. The tax collector therefore appeared to him to have had more to bear than the Pharisee had. He went down more justified than the Pharisee did, only because of the fact he was humble.
—**St. Ephrem the Syrian,** *Commentary on Tatian's Diatessaron*

The foolish Pharisee stood there bold and broad, lifting up his eyes without a qualm, bearing witness to himself and boastful. The other feels shame for his conduct. He is afraid of his judge. He beats his breast. He confesses his offenses. He shows his illness to the physician, and he prays that he will have mercy. What is the result? Let us hear what the judge says. He says, "This man went down to his house justified rather than the other."

—St. Cyril of Alexandria, *Commentary on Luke*

Practical Pointers for Bible Discussion Groups

A Bible discussion group is another key that can help us unlock the treasures of God's word. Participating in a discussion or study group—whether through a parish, a prayer group, or a neighborhood—offers us the opportunity to grow not only in our love for God's word but also in our love for one another. We don't have to be trained Scripture scholars to benefit from discussing and studying the Bible together. Bible study groups provide environments in which we can worship and pray together and strengthen our relationships with other Christians. The following guidelines can help a group get started and run smoothly.

Getting Started

- Decide on a regular time and place to meet. Meeting on a regular basis allows the group to maintain continuity without losing momentum from the previous discussion.

- Set a time limit for each session. An hour and a half is a reasonable length of time in which to have a rewarding discussion on the material contained in each of the sessions in this guide. However, the group may find that a longer time is even more advantageous. If it is necessary to limit the meeting to an hour, select sections of the material that are of greatest interest to the group.

- Designate a moderator or facilitator to lead the discussions and keep the meetings on schedule. This person's role is to help preserve good group dynamics by keeping the discussion on track. He or she should help ensure that no one monopolizes the session and that each person—especially shy or quiet individuals—is offered an opportunity to speak. The group may want to ask members to take turns moderating the sessions.

- Provide enough copies of the study guide for each member of the group, and ask everyone to bring a Bible to the meetings. Each session's Scripture text and related passages for reflection are printed in full in the guides, but you will find that a Bible is helpful for looking up other passages and cross-references. The translation provided in this guide is the New Revised Standard Version (Catholic Edition). You may also want to refer to other translations—for example, the New American Bible or the New Jerusalem Bible—to gain additional insights into the text.

- Try to stay faithful to your commitment and attend as many sessions as possible. Not only does regular participation provide coherence and consistency to the group discussions, it also demonstrates that members value one another and are committed to sharing their lives with one another.

Session Dynamics

- Read the material for each session in advance and take time to consider the questions and your answers to them. The single most important key to any successful Bible study is having everyone prepared to participate.

- As a courtesy to all members of your group, try to begin and end each session on schedule. Being prompt respects the other commitments of the members and allows enough time for discussion.

If the group still has more to discuss at the end of the allotted time, consider continuing the discussion at the next meeting.

- Open the sessions with prayer. A different person could have the responsibility of leading the opening prayer at each session. The prayer could be a spontaneous one, a traditional prayer such as the Our Father, or one that relates to the topic of that particular meeting. The members of the group might also want to begin some of the meetings with a song or hymn. Whatever you choose, ask the Holy Spirit to guide your discussion and study of the Scripture text presented in that session.

- Contribute actively to the discussion. Let the members of the group get to know you, but try to stick to the topic so that you won't divert the discussion from its purpose. And resist the temptation to monopolize the conversation, so that everyone will have an opportunity to learn from one another.

- Listen attentively to everyone in the group. Show respect for the other members and their contributions. Encourage, support, and affirm them as they share. Remember that many questions have more than one answer and that the experience of everyone in the group can be enriched by considering a variety of viewpoints.

- If you disagree with someone's observation or answer to a question, do so gently and respectfully, in a way that shows that you value the person who made the comment, and then explain your own point of view. For example, rather than say, "You're wrong!" or, "That's ridiculous!" try something like, "I think I see what you're getting at, but I think that Jesus was saying something different in this passage." Be careful to avoid sounding aggressive or argumentative. Then, watch to see how the subsequent discussion unfolds. Who knows? You may come away with a new and deeper perspective.

- Don't be afraid of pauses and reflective moments of silence during the session. People may need some time to think about a question before putting their thoughts into words.

- Maintain and respect confidentiality within the group. Safeguard the privacy and dignity of each member by not repeating what has been shared during the discussion session unless you have been given permission to do so. That way everyone will get the greatest benefit out of the group by feeling comfortable enough to share on a deep, personal level.

- End the session with prayer. Thank God for what you have learned through the discussion, and ask him to help you integrate it into your life.

The Lord blesses all our efforts to come closer to him. As you spend time preparing for and meeting with your small group, be confident in the knowledge that Christ will fill you with wisdom, insight, and grace and the ability to see him at work in your daily life.

Sources and Acknowledgments

Session 1: The Good Samaritan

Page 19:
Herman Hendrickx, *The Parables of Jesus* (London: Geoffrey Chapman, 1986), 90–91.

Pages 25–26:
Louise Perrotta, "The Grace to Be Taken by Surprise," *God's Word Today,* October 1996, 46–47. Reprinted with permission of the author.

Page 30:
Jerome, *Homily on Psalm 14 (15),* quoted in *Ancient Christian Commentary on Scripture: Luke,* ed. Arthur A. Just, Jr. (Downers Grove, IL: InterVarsity Press, 2003), 179. Copyright © 2003 by the Institute of Classical Christian Studies (ICCS), Thomas C. Oden and Arthur A. Just, Jr. Used with permission of InterVarsity Press, P.O. Box 1400, Downers Grove, IL 60515. www.ivpress.com.

Origen, *Homilies on the Gospel of Luke* 34.3, 9, quoted in *Ancient Christian Commentary on Scripture: Luke,* ed. Arthur A. Just, Jr. (Downers Grove, IL: InterVarsity Press, 2003), 180. Copyright © 2003 by the Institute of Classical Christian Studies (ICCS), Thomas C. Oden and Arthur A. Just, Jr. Used with permission of InterVarsity Press, P.O. Box 1400, Downers Grove, IL 60515. www.ivpress.com.

Session 2: The Lost Sheep

Page 33:
John Paul II, *Homily at Mass at the Trans World Dome,* St. Louis, 27 January 1999, no. 2, www.vatican.va/holy_father/john_paul_ii/travels/documents/hf_jp-ii_hom_27011999_stlouis_en.html.

Page 37:
John Paul II, *Homily on the 25th Anniversary of His Pontificate,* 16 October 2003, no. 2, www.vatican.va/holy_father/john_paul_ii/homilies/2003/documents/hf_jp-ii_hom_20031016_xxv-pontificate_en.html.

Page 38:
John Paul II, *Homily to the Poor Clares of Albano,* 14 August 1979, quoted in *The Navarre Bible: The Gospel of St. Matthew,* with a commentary by the members of the Faculty of Theology of the University of Navarre (Blackrock, Ireland: Four Courts Press, 1993), 164.

Page 40:
Ambrose, *Exposition of the Gospel of Luke,* 7.209, quoted in *Ancient Christian Commentary on Scripture: Luke,* ed. Arthur A. Just, Jr. (Downers Grove, IL: InterVarsity Press, 2003), 245. Copyright © 2003 by the Institute of Classical Christian Studies (ICCS), Thomas C. Oden and Arthur A. Just, Jr. Used with permission of InterVarsity Press, P.O. Box 1400, Downers Grove, IL 60515. www.ivpress.com.

Gregory the Great, *Homily 34,* quoted in *Forty Gospel Homilies,* trans. Dom David Hurst (Kalamazoo, MI: Cistercian Publications, 1990), 282–283.

Page 42:
Terrie Belleci, quoted in *God's Word Today,* July 1998, 40.
Reprinted with permission of the author.

Pages 43–44:
Phillip Keller, *A Shepherd Looks at Psalm 23* (Grand Rapids,
MI: Zondervan Publishing House, 1979), 62–64. Copyright ©
1970 by W. Phillip Keller. Reprinted with permission of The
Zondervan Corporation.

SESSION 3: THE LABORERS IN THE VINEYARD

Page 47:
Jan Lambrecht, *Out of the Treasure: The Parables in the Gospel of
Matthew* (Louvain, Belgium: Peeters Press, 1998), 79.

Page 52:
George Smiga, *God's Word Today,* February 2005, 18.

Page 55:
John Paul II, *On the Vocation and the Mission of the Lay
Faithful in the Church and in the World*, 30 December 1988,
nos. 2–3, 58, www.vatican.va/holy_father/john_paul_ii/apost_
exhortations/documents/hf_jp-ii_exh_30121988_christifideles-
laici_en.html.

Pages 57–58:
Marilyn Gustin, *How to Read and Pray the Parables* (Liguori,
MO: Liguori Publications, 1992), 55–56. Copyright © 1992
by Liguori Publications. Reprinted with permission of Liguori
Publications, Liguori, MO 63057.

Session 4: The Treasure and the Pearl

Page 61:
Frank Sheed, *To Know Christ Jesus* (San Francisco: Ignatius Press, 1992), 217.

Page 66:
Gregory the Great, *Hom. in Ev.*, 11, 2, quoted in Thomas Aquinas, *Catena Aurea*, Gospel of Matthew, chapter 13, www.ccel.org/a/aquinas/catena/Matthew/ch13.htm.

Irenaeus, *Against Heresies*, bk. 4, ch. 26, §1, quoted in *The Ante-Nicene Fathers*, vol. 1, ed. Alexander Roberts and James Donaldson (New Advent, 1996), www.newadvent.org/fathers/0103426.htm.

Augustine, *Quaest. in Matt.*, *q. 13*, quoted in Thomas Aquinas, *Catena Aurea*, Gospel of Matthew, chapter 13, www.ccel.org/a/aquinas/catena/Matthew/ch13.htm.

Page 69:
George Montague, *Companion God: A Cross-Cultural Commentary on the Gospel of Matthew* (New York: Paulist Press, 1989), 61.

John Paul II, *The Splendor of Truth*, 6 August 1993, no. 66, www.vatican.va/edocs/ENG0222/_INDEX.HTM.

Page 71:
Pliny, *Natural History,* quoted in "History of Pearls," www.ama-pearls.com/Main%20Frameset/Historical%20Interest/Historial%20Interest.htm.

Pages 72–73:
Bishop Kenneth Untener, *Homily*, 28 July 2002, www.saginaw.
org/untener/homilies_2002/homily2002_0728.htm. Reprinted
with permission of the Diocese of Saginaw.

Session 5: The Rich Fool

Page 75:
George Martin, *God's Word Today*, February 1995, 7.

Page 82:
Paul VI, *On the Development of Peoples*, 26 March 1967, no.
19, www.vatican.va/holy_father/paul_vi/encyclicals/documents/
hf_p-vi_enc_26031967_populorum_en.html.

Page 85:
Respect Life: . . . In the Words of Mother Teresa of Calcutta, ed.
Corinne Hart (Los Angeles: Franciscan Communications, 1982),
17.

Page 86:
*Love: A Fruit Always in Season—Daily Meditations by Mother
Teresa of Calcutta,* ed. Dorothy S. Hunt (San Francisco: Ignatius
Press, 1987), 205.

Session 6: The Pharisee and the Tax Collector

Page 89:
Augustine, *Sermon 351.1,* quoted in *Ancient Christian Commen-
tary on Scripture: Luke,* ed. Arthur A. Just, Jr. (Downers Grove,
IL: InterVarsity Press, 2003), 279. Copyright © 2003 by the Insti-
tute of Classical Christian Studies (ICCS), Thomas C. Oden and
Arthur A. Just, Jr. Used with permission of InterVarsity Press, P.O.
Box 1400, Downers Grove, IL 60515. www.ivpress.com.

Pages 93–94:
John Jay Hughes, *Stories Jesus Told: Modern Meditations on the Parables* (Liguori, MO: Liguori Publications, 1999), 38–39. Reprinted with permission of Liguori Publications, Liguori, MO 63057.

Page 99:
Basil the Great, *On Humility*, quoted in *Ancient Christian Commentary on Scripture: Luke*, ed. Arthur A. Just, Jr. (Downers Grove, IL: InterVarsity Press, 2003), 280. Copyright © 2003 by the Institute of Classical Christian Studies (ICCS), Thomas C. Oden and Arthur A. Just, Jr. Used with permission of InterVarsity Press, P.O. Box 1400, Downers Grove, IL 60515. www.ivpress.com.

Ephrem the Syrian, *Commentary on Tatian's Diatessaron 15.24*, quoted in *Ancient Christian Commentary on Scripture: Luke*, ed. Arthur A. Just, Jr. (Downers Grove, IL: InterVarsity Press, 2003), 280. Copyright © 2003 by the Institute of Classical Christian Studies (ICCS), Thomas C. Oden and Arthur A. Just, Jr. Used with permission of InterVarsity Press, P.O. Box 1400, Downers Grove, IL 60515. www.ivpress.com.

Page 100:
Cyril of Alexandria, *Commentary on Luke, Homily 120*, quoted in *Ancient Christian Commentary on Scripture: Luke*, ed. Arthur A. Just, Jr. (Downers Grove, IL: InterVarsity Press, 2003), 280. Copyright © 2003 by the Institute of Classical Christian Studies (ICCS), Thomas C. Oden and Arthur A. Just, Jr. Used with permission of InterVarsity Press, P.O. Box 1400, Downers Grove, IL 60515. www.ivpress.com.

Also by Jeanne Kun

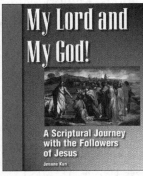

Item# BDSCE5

My Lord and My God
A Scriptural Journey with the Followers of Jesus

My Lord and My God! A Scriptural Journey with the Followers of Jesus is based on ten gospel characters who encountered Jesus in a life-changing way. Simon Peter, Bartimaeus, Mary of Bethany, Joseph of Arimathea, Thomas—and others—show just how diverse the faces of discipleship are.

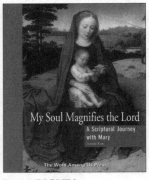

Item# BIGVE3

My Soul Magnifies the Lord
A Scriptural Journey with Mary

Follow in the footsteps of the first disciple of Jesus—his mother Mary. This unique book focuses on ten important gospel scenes in the life of the Blessed Virgin Mary, from her *fiat* at the Annunciation to her presence in the upper room at Pentecost.

"By presenting the milestones of Mary's life as recorded in the Bible, this Scripture study can do a great deal to increase its readers' faith and humbleness of heart."
National Catholic Register

"An enticing guide to prayer."
Bible Today